THE
SELF-MANAGED
DEVELOPMENT POCKETBOOK

By Fiona Elsa Dent

Drawings by Phil Hailstone

"Pocket-sized and powerful – an essential comprehensive guide to the key discipline of self-managed development."
Tom O'Connor, Head of Knowledge Management Systems, BG plc.

"Self-managed development is all about taking responsibility and reflecting, both before and after action - key issues in the changing and dynamic business environment. Fiona Dent's book is practical, thought provoking and, above all, encourages us to take responsibility for our own outcomes."
Mike Brent, Senior Associate, M.I.L. Institute, Sweden.

Published by:
Management Pocketbooks Ltd
14 East Street, Alresford, Hants SO24 9EE, U.K.
Tel: +44 (0)1962 735573   Fax: +44 (0)1962 733637
E-mail: pocketbks@aol.com
Web: www.pocketbook.co.uk

This edition published 1999 Reprinted 2000

© Fiona Elsa Dent 1999

ISBN 1 870471 66 0

British Library Cataloguing-in-Publication Data – A catalogue record for this book
is available from the British Library.

Printed in U.K.

CONTENTS

INTRODUCTION 1
You and your future, new and exciting challenges, defining self-managed development

WHY SELF-MANAGED DEVELOPMENT? 7
Why organisations are incorporating self-managed development as part of their HR strategy, a case study, obstacles, benefits, getting started

A MODEL FOR SELF-MANAGED DEVELOPMENT 23
Self-managed development must be an integrated and interactive process, as our model shows

EXTERNAL FACTORS OF SELF-MANAGED DEVELOPMENT 27
How the business's objectives and other external factors impact on your development, and the role other people (the 'learning network') will play

SELF-ANALYSIS 51
Making effective decisions about your future hinges on raising self-awareness through SWOT, job analysis (so-called 'job tree'), skills audits, performance reviews, etc

REFLECTION 75
Reflecting on your perceptions will reveal new choices and opportunities for the future; this chapter shows you what to ask yourself, what to ask others, how to structure and receive feedback, and how to visualise the future

ACTION PLANNING 93
Setting objectives and measuring your commitment and motivation

SUMMARY 103

INTRODUCTION

AUTHOR'S NOTE

As a self-development experience, writing this pocketbook has been one of my most challenging yet satisfying experiences.

The idea of writing a whole book by myself was particularly daunting - especially as I had a self-fulfilling prophecy about my writing skills (or, to be more precise, my lack of them!). Previously I had co-authored a book with two others and this did much to challenge this self-perceived weakness. However, I always felt that the real challenge would be to write a book completely by myself.

This done, perhaps the next challenge will be to tackle a novel!

INTRODUCTION

GETTING ON IN THE WORLD

George Bernard Shaw said:

"The people who get on in this world are the people who get up and look for the circumstances they want and, if they can't find them, make them."

A slightly idealistic statement, perhaps. However, it may be that self-managed development is a way of helping people to find or make the right circumstances!

YOU & YOUR FUTURE

You may be asking yourself: 'Why self-managed development when there are so many other things in my life?'.

BUT

- Are you really happy with what you have achieved in life and work so far?
  Could you be doing more?
- Do you want to do more?
- Are there things in life that you've always wanted to do but never quite got round to?
- Are there opportunities you haven't taken?

Now is the time to start doing something about it. Self-managed development is all about **you** taking responsibility for **your** future!

NEW & EXCITING CHALLENGES

Many organisations are incorporating self-managed development into their management development strategy. They actively want to encourage people to take more control of, and responsibility for, their own development. After all, people are an organisation's most important asset.

This, of course, does not mean that the organisation abdicates its responsibility for its people's development; in some ways it creates a more complex situation for human resources people. For the individual, as a self-developer, new and exciting challenges exist.

This pocketbook gives an overview of the self-managed development process and a range of practical exercises to help people get started. I have also included some case studies of people who are successful self-developers and who are committed to the process.

DEFINING SELF-MANAGED DEVELOPMENT

Self-managed development is the process whereby **you** take responsibility for, and control of, your own development.

As long ago as the 16th century, Galileo said:

"You cannot teach a man anything. You can only help him discover it in himself."

WHY SELF-MANAGED DEVELOPMENT?

WHY ARE ORGANISATIONS DOING IT?

Typically, human resource professionals cite one or more of the reasons given here and on the following pages for incorporating self-managed development into their HR strategy.

1. Changes in career patterns, both from an organisational and individual perspective, involving some of the following:

● Organisations are employing more rigorous performance measures

● There are shorter, less predictable career paths

● Increasingly, portfolio v corporate careers

● There is greater mobility between companies

● Management talent is identified early and promotion follows

● Increased job insecurity

Dominic Cadbury recently said:

"There is no such thing as a career path, there is only crazy paving and you have to lay it yourself."

WHY SELF-MANAGED DEVELOPMENT?

WHY ARE ORGANISATIONS DOING IT?

2. Individuals in organisations are being called upon to develop new managerial skills and capabilities:

- Ability to 'helicopter vision' and use their imagination
- The move from specialist to generalist - the individual who has a holistic view of the organisation
- Exceptional process and people skills - teamworking, influencing and interpersonal skills
- Leadership skills and the ability to cope with change and complexity
- Sensitivity to cultural differences and diversity

WHY ARE ORGANISATIONS DOING IT?

3. The ability to cope with change, both at an organisational and individual level, is something that we all have to deal with in today's business environment:

- **Individual change**
  - continuous learning and development to keep up-to-date
  - the need to acquire recognisable transferable skills
  - the expectation that individuals 'own' their own development

- **Organisational change**
  - development of individuals enhances their ability to cope with organisational change

- **'The Learning Organisation'**
  - an organisation's ability to learn faster than its competitors is its only sustainable competitive advantage

WHY SELF-MANAGED DEVELOPMENT?

ORGANISATIONAL CHANGE

The environment facing people in organisations is rapidly changing and the features of organisational life in the past are no longer certain for the future:

Yesterday		Tomorrow
• Hierarchies and control	➡	Matrix management and empowerment
• Organisations develop their people	➡	Development owned by individuals
• Progression 'up the ladder' one step at a time	➡	Progression based on merit
• Career growth	➡	Personal growth/'portfolio' working
• Focus on training	➡	Focus on learning

CAREER CHANGES

Changes to organisational life lead to changes in the way people manage their careers:

Yesterday	Tomorrow
• One organisation/job/career	➝ Multiple organisations/jobs/careers
• Upward progression	➝ Many alternative career paths
• Formal education	➝ Continuous learning
• Development decided for you	➝ You take responsibility
• Job security	➝ Portfolio careers and employability

CASE STUDY: SIMON'S STORY

Simon left school at 19 and went straight into officer cadet training at Sandhurst. He then spent eight years following a traditional army career and, at a fairly young age, reached the level of captain. Sadly, a knee injury restricted his ability to undertake field work, which was his preference and, having done a few 'desk' jobs, he resigned his commission in 1990.

Having left the army, Simon was keen to find a suitable and satisfying alternative career. He also quickly realised that - in contrast to the army, where many (if not all) development decisions are made for you - in 'civvy street' things are a bit different and it was now down to him.

CASE STUDY: SIMON'S STORY

With the help of Stewart (whom he now recognises as a bit of a mentor) and other contacts, he began to define and recognise the wide range of skills and competences he had developed during his years in the army. Reflecting back over the eight years, he identified that he had gained experience in many areas which could help him in his future career - skills in leadership, people management, decision-making, problem-solving, influencing, presenting and developing others.

In discussion with Stewart, among others, he decided to pursue a career in training and development. His first two opportunities proved to be superb learning experiences. One involved working for just over a year with a training consultancy, where Simon's selling skills were developed, but frustration set in when he wasn't allowed to 'see things through'.

CASE STUDY: SIMON'S STORY

The other major learning experience was a brief period of self-employment. When this didn't work out, he recognised that he needed to develop computer skills, and so he bought a PC and taught himself word processing, database management and desk-top publishing skills - all of which were to prove useful in the future!

Simon again enlisted Stewart's help, and applied and was accepted for a job as training manager for a large Middle Eastern airline based in Dubai. During his time with this company he has gained much experience including setting up, with a contact, his own training consultancy. His colleague, Brian, has proved to be a superb learning partner and he, plus other contacts, have helped Simon to reach the decision that he is ready to move on again.

However, a lack of qualifications is now proving to be a disadvantage so he is investigating various options in order to help himself move ahead!

SIMON'S STORY

KEY SELF-DEVELOPMENT ISSUES

What makes Simon's story interesting from a self-managed development perspective?

- Firstly, having the guts to recognise that the army was no longer satisfying and meeting his career needs
- Recognising that he needed help and support to sort out his next move
- Spending time analysing and reflecting on his skills (What were the transferable skills?)
- Taking the opportunity to develop new skills, both on the job – his selling skills - and in his own time – his computing skills
- Taking risks in new areas (consultancy and self-employment) yet facing up to the issue when neither worked out and moving on to pastures new
- Making opportunities for new experiences: setting up his own consultancy using established skills
- And now, still recognising that he needs formal qualifications to get further

So, for Simon, leaving the safe environment of the army, where he had been very successful and had an excellent track-record, was a challenge he faced up to by taking responsibility for his own development and future, and kept going even when things were very tough.

PROBLEMS

While there are many reasons for organisations and individuals to adopt self-managed development processes, they are not without their problems. Any person or organisation who intends to adopt this approach as a development philosophy must be aware of the challenges as well as the benefits:

- The day-to-day demands of any job can sabotage the learning opportunities
- Maintaining energy, enthusiasm and commitment to the whole process can be demanding upon individuals and organisations alike
- Lack of support from others, especially senior and line management
- The difficulties involved in measuring the effectiveness of the process
- Getting started in the first place!

ROLE CHANGES

Organisations, which have promoted self-managed development as a development philosophy, have also made certain role changes in terms of responsibilities for development:

- **Organisation** - as provider of information and resources

- **Line manager** - as facilitator, coach, mentor, learning partner

- **Employee** - as taker and maker of development opportunities, who then applies new skills

THE MANAGERIAL JIGSAW

Gone are the days when the individuals in an organisation could content themselves with one role or specialism. The current reality facing individuals in organisational life is such that they have to be 'multifaceted'. The reality is a bit like a jigsaw where people have to develop the skills and competence to be effective in all four roles:

Specialist   Generalist   Networker   Independent

THE INDIVIDUAL IN THE ORGANISATION

So, what does being effective in all four roles actually mean?

- **Specialist** - everyone must be a specialist in something (for instance, in accounts or information technology, in word processing or in personnel, etc)

- **Generalist** – increasingly, people must have sufficient general business knowledge to be able to work in multi-functional teams and hold their own in discussions on many business issues

- **Networker** - the ability to work in teams and to communicate effectively outside your own particular work group or area is becoming vital

- **Independent** - the successful person in organisational life today will be an independent individual who will take responsibility for him/herself in all aspects of organisational life

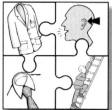

The challenge is fitting all the pieces together!

WHY SELF-MANAGED DEVELOPMENT?

WHY YOU SHOULD DO IT

There are many reasons for people to take responsibility for their own development. Some of the key ones are:

- ✔ For improved career management
- ✔ To improve current ability
- ✔ To develop knowledge or skill
- ✔ To manage a life change
- ✔ Because the person wants to take control

Remember, ultimately YOU are responsible for your own development!

GETTING STARTED

ACTIVITY IDEA

Once you have decided that you want to manage your own development, you should develop a system for recording your thoughts, ideas and plans. So, this first activity idea involves you in **creating a development log**.

First of all, think about how you like to learn and how best you can record your progress, thoughts and ideas.

You may find a simple notebook or record cards sufficient for your needs, or you could build your log into your personal organiser or even create a development log on your PC. Remember, whatever approach you choose the only important thing is that it works for **you**.

Use this log to record important thoughts and ideas, which may be prompted by the activities and other elements of this book.

A MODEL FOR
SELF-MANAGED DEVELOPMENT

INTERACTIVE PROCESS

The process of self-managed development has to be an integrated and interactive process: integrated in the sense that it must link to other organisational processes, and interactive in that it must involve others.
The model here shows the various processes involved.

A MODEL FOR SELF-MANAGED DEVELOPMENT

EXTERNAL FACTORS

The outer rim of the self-managed development model indicates four external factors that an individual may take account of and involve in managing his or her own development.

Business objectives are key to the whole process. Having a good understanding of your organisation's strategy and objectives will help you to put your own learning and development needs into a context.

Learning relationships refer to all the people with whom you develop learning relationships and who help in your self-managed development.

Career objectives should be considered, even though these may change over time. However, having some sort of career plan will help you to focus on the important aspects of your development.

Learning activities are the learning processes you take part in in order to develop your skills and knowledge.

A MODEL FOR SELF-MANAGED DEVELOPMENT

PERSONAL FACTORS

The inner core of the model shows the three key elements which you, as an individual, must do in order to effectively get started on the process of self-managed development.

- **Self-analysis** involves any process of examining your current range of strengths, weaknesses, skills, competences, etc

- **Reflection** involves you in reviewing, possibly with another person or a group of people, where you are now and where you want to get to

- **Action planning** is when you take all the analysis and reflection and begin to make sense of it by deciding what you are going to do, how you intend to develop and when you are going to do it

While this part of the process is almost completely down to **you**, the individual, the outer frame, to a large extent, involves others. Indeed, the whole process of self-managed development cannot be done in isolation. As a minimum, you should involve others by developing learning relationships. For even greater effectiveness, your organisation can be involved by offering support, guidance and resources.

EXTERNAL FACTORS OF
SELF-MANAGED DEVELOPMENT

EXTERNAL FACTORS

BUSINESS OBJECTIVES

Understanding the business objectives of your organisation, business unit, department or, even, team can help you to put your self-managed development into context and help you to prioritise your self-development objectives. Focusing on the following areas will help you to determine what is important in terms of your business life:

- The overall purpose of your business
- The environment in which your organisation operates
- The market in which your organisation operates
- The key business challenges facing your organisation now and in the future
- The long-term business objectives (say, 5-year plans)
- The short-term business plans (the next 12 months)

You must decide whether to focus on the whole organisation or a smaller subset which would be more appropriate for your self-managed development.

EXTERNAL FACTORS

BUSINESS OBJECTIVES

ACTIVITY IDEA

It is worth noting in your log some information associated with your business life. So, consider the following and make appropriate notes for your particular needs:

- The overall purpose of your business
- The purpose of your business area
- The key business issues which will affect your self-managed development
    - in the short-term (say, next 12 months)
    - in the long-term (5–10 years)

EXTERNAL FACTORS

CAREER OBJECTIVES

Obviously, your career objectives will change over time and will be affected by many external factors. It is important, therefore, to reflect on the past, present and future and to have a clear idea of how you got to where you are now and where you plan to get to.

- Review your education and how it has contributed to your career so far
- Reflect on your first job and how it has affected your career path so far
- Question who or what has affected your career decisions
- Describe your career successes so far
- Describe any career disappointments
- If there were no constraints (family, geographical, qualifications, etc) ask yourself what your dream job/career would be
- Taking account of present realities, describe your current career objectives

EXTERNAL FACTORS

CAREER OBJECTIVES
ACTIVITY IDEA

Allocate one section of your learning log to review your career and job experience to date. Make notes about the following:

- Career successes so far
- Career disappointments so far
- Career objectives for the future

LEARNING RELATIONSHIPS

Developing appropriate learning relationships is vital to the success of self-managed development, both from the individual's and the organisation's viewpoint.

The individual's viewpoint

It seems paradoxical, but self-managed development cannot be done totally on your own. Most people develop a range of 'learning relationships', with people who can challenge, help, support and even inspire.

The organisation's viewpoint

The organisation's responsibility for learning relationships involves encouraging and enabling, to ensure that self-managed development is regarded as a legitimate organisational process and seen as part of an effective human resource strategy.

LEARNING RELATIONSHIPS

As an encourager and enabler, your organisation can provide some or all of the following:

- Overt support for any self-managed development programme
- Training and education for appropriate people (senior managers, line managers, HR specialists, etc) to ensure that they are very clear about their role and responsibilities
- Provision of a range of learning materials and resources
- A system of recognition for progress and achievements
- Encouragement of organisational specialists (eg: finance people, marketing people) to act as coaches and advisers

EXTERNAL FACTORS

ACTIVITY IDEA

Consider the support mechanisms, which are available in your organisation and make a note in your learning log. Then reflect upon these and note down the ones you have used.

Are there any additional support mechanisms you could be using? Note down what they are and how you could be using them.

LEARNING RELATIONSHIPS

As a self-developer you may well have developed relationships with many people who assist you in your self-managed development. Typical relationships can be categorised as follows:

Coach

Mentor

Role model

Counsellor

Learning partner

Learning support group

Collectively, the people with whom you develop learning relationships are known as your learning network.

LEARNING RELATIONSHIPS

LEARNING NETWORK

Each of us will have our own learning network – namely, the various people who have helped us to learn, grow and develop over the years. A useful way to examine your learning network is to create a mind map of all the people with whom you have had learning relationships in your life.

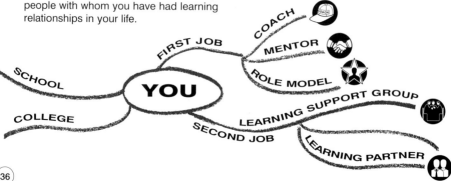

LEARNING RELATIONSHIPS

ACTIVITY IDEA

Think about all the people with whom you have developed learning relationships over the years and draw (like a mind map) your learning network. Put your name in the circle below and then add branches and annotate them with the name of the person with whom you have had a learning relationship.

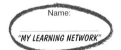

Name:

"MY LEARNING NETWORK"

LEARNING RELATIONSHIPS

RELATIONSHIP SKILLS

Each learning relationship will offer slightly different benefits and the role of each relationship will differ. However, to be really effective in any of the learning relationship roles described on the following pages, certain skills are necessary:

- Excellent communication skills
  - listening
  - questioning
  - testing understanding
  - summarising
- Ability to challenge
- Empathy
- Influencing skills
- Discretion

LEARNING RELATIONSHIPS

THE COACH

How do each of the relationship roles differ? Let's define each role and look at the key features each offers the learner, beginning with the 'coach'.

The dictionary definition of a coach is 'a private tutor', often someone who is assigned to help you. This is probably as good a definition as any, but what special features would a coach provide you with?

Typically, a coach is someone who can help you develop a particular skill, competence or area of knowledge. A coach need not necessarily be an expert or the best, simply someone who is knowledgeable in a certain area and has the skills mentioned earlier.

A good example might be to think of a football coach. Often, those who are cited as the best coaches were not always the best players.

(39)

LEARNING RELATIONSHIPS

THE MENTOR

The mentor is an experienced and trusted counsellor who will provide guidance and advice or simply a discreet ear.

Typically, an effective mentor-learner relationship will be developed through mutual respect and interest in one another. You, the learner, will often be instrumental in setting up the relationship.

Mentors frequently have one or more of the following characteristics:

- Greater seniority than yourself in the organisation
- More experience than yourself in your chosen career
- Similar interests to yours, but with more experience
- The ability, in your eyes, to be a 'wise counsel'

LEARNING RELATIONSHIPS

THE ROLE MODEL

The role model is often someone you admire from afar, someone who is:

- Famous
- Written about frequently
- More senior than you in your organisation

The role model provides you
with a learning relationship
at a distance - not a
personal relationship.
That person will be
someone who
inspires you and who
you would like to
emulate in some way.

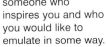

LEARNING RELATIONSHIPS
THE COUNSELLOR

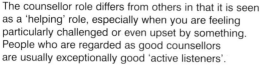

The counsellor role differs from others in that it is seen as a 'helping' role, especially when you are feeling particularly challenged or even upset by something. People who are regarded as good counsellors are usually exceptionally good 'active listeners'.

The counsel such people provide is often associated with problem analysis, helping you to think a problem through and then helping you come up with a course of action for solving the problem or moving on.

EXTERNAL FACTORS

LEARNING RELATIONSHIPS

THE LEARNING PARTNER

A learning partner is a like-minded person who may have similar learning and development needs to yourself. Or, perhaps, it is someone with whom you enjoy working and you find that you act as foils for one another, learning as your relationship develops.

In addition to the skills necessary for effective learning relationships, certain features are important for effective learning partnerships. These are:

- Trust
- Honesty
- Openness

LEARNING RELATIONSHIPS
THE LEARNING PARTNER (cont'd)

Meeting together in learning partnerships can be all the more effective if the following process (or a similar process) is agreed and adopted:

- Agree the subject

- Agree the goal of the discussion

- Agree which partner will be the focus of the discussion this time (usually this person will instigate the meeting)

- The listener should encourage but not interrupt

- When you think the learner has said everything, ask that person to re-examine his/her goal

- Ask the learner to summarise the next steps or plan of action

Do not attempt to analyse the session!

LEARNING RELATIONSHIPS
THE LEARNING SUPPORT GROUP

This is any group of which you are a member that provides you with learning and developmental experiences. The groups can be official or unofficial, inside or outside the organisation, professional or self-help, etc.

The word **support** is very important in this context as the concept of the learning support group is such that the members are supportive of one another. This does not mean being nice to each other but, rather, providing a challenging environment in which mutual respect exists and the full range of learning relationship skills is used.

LEARNING RELATIONSHIPS

THE LEARNING SUPPORT GROUP (cont'd)

By adopting the following process or a similar one, learning support group meetings can be very much more focused and useful:

- Agree the meeting objective

- Agree the stop time for the meeting

- Start the meeting positively by asking everyone to describe something they have achieved since the last meeting

- During the initial discussion, allow everyone equal, uninterrupted 'air time' to state their views on the topic (usually 5-10 mins each)

- Summarise each person's views on a flipchart prior to open discussion

- Open discussion for a timed period

- Agree action points and the way ahead

LEARNING RELATIONSHIPS

ACTIVITY IDEA

Refer back to the previous activity (page 37, your learning network). Try to categorise each learning relationship and annotate the type of relationship beside the person's name on your learning network.

You might also like to add to your chart some or all of the following information:

- Length of time you have had the relationship
- Work or non work-related relationship
- Job or profession of the person
- Age of the person

Now examine your chart: does this tell you anything about your learning style and the people with whom you prefer to interact when learning?

LEARNING ACTIVITIES

There are many day-to-day activities in which we all take part that can provide opportunities for learning. For instance:

- Project work
- Secondment
- Computer-based learning (even surfing the Internet!)
- Structured reading
- Attending conferences
- On-the-job coaching
- Work shadowing
- Action learning sets
- Job swaps
- Distance learning
- Interactive video
- Training courses and workshops
- Video watching (not only training ones; sometimes feature films can be educational!)
- Giving a presentation
- Chairing a meeting

The important thing about a learning activity is that you have to make it one!

LEARNING ACTIVITIES
ACTIVITY IDEA

Reflect back over the last few weeks or
months and list in your learning log all
the activities or experiences you have
had which you can now regard as
learning experiences.

LEARNING ACTIVITIES

ACTIVITY IDEA

Now reflect on each of the activities or experiences that you have listed in the previous exercise and ask yourself what you learned from each. You should note down the answers in your learning log.

Having done this, reflect on the notes you have made and ask yourself: 'What does this tell me about the way I like to learn?'.

Self-analysis

RAISING SELF-AWARENESS

The process of self-analysis involves you in a wide variety of different possibilities and opportunities for raising self-awareness. The idea here is to gather sufficient information in order to make effective decisions about future objectives for your self-managed development.
By examining your current range of strengths, weaknesses, skills and competences, you will gain a clearer idea of 'who you are' and 'what you've got'.

RAISING SELF-AWARENESS

There are many different ways of raising self-awareness through self-analysis.
Some quite simple ways are:

- SWOT analysis
- Current job analysis
- Questionnaire completion:
  - self-assessment of skills or competences
  - personality questionnaires
  - questionnaires which focus on particular skill areas (for instance, how you deal with conflict, how you influence, what your team type is, how you learn, etc)
- Performance review
- Discussions with colleagues to gain feedback

SWOT ANALYSIS

SWOT analysis involves a process of examining your **S**trengths, **W**eaknesses, **O**pportunities and **T**hreats in relation to either your personal or career development.

Under each heading you should examine the following:

Strengths   - the things you are good at

Weaknesses   - the things you do not handle well or cannot handle

Opportunities   - those factors or changes external to yourself that will affect you positively (for instance, possible organisational changes, geographical moves, soon to be gaining a qualification, etc)

Threats   - those factors or changes external to yourself that may affect you adversely (for instance, loss of a customer, a new competitor enters your market, etc)

SWOT ANALYSIS
ACTIVITY IDEA

You should undertake this activity prior to completing any other form of self-analysis, as it is best to do this with a completely open mind before you are affected by any other external factors.

Split a page in your learning log into four:

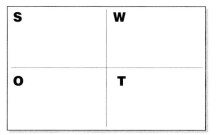

S	W
O	T

Using the instructions on the previous page, note down everything that you consider to be your strengths, weaknesses, opportunities and threats.

A JOB TREE

Undertaking a detailed job analysis of your current role can also help you to gain a better overview of 'who you are' and 'what you've got'. One way of doing this is to create a job tree, as described on the following pages.

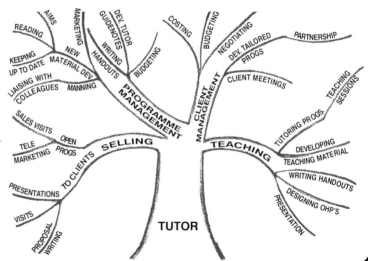

PROGRAMME MANAGEMENT

- AIMS
- READING
- KEEPING UP TO DATE
- NEW MATERIAL DEV
- LIAISING WITH COLLEAGUES
- MANNING
- MARKETING
- DEV. TUTOR GUIDENOTES
- WRITING HANDOUTS
- BUDGETING

CLIENT MANAGEMENT

- COSTING
- BUDGETING
- NEGOTIATING
- DEV. TAILORED PROGS
- PARTNERSHIP
- CLIENT MEETINGS

TEACHING

- TUTORING PROGS
- TEACHING SESSIONS
- DEVELOPING TEACHING MATERIAL
- WRITING HANDOUTS
- DESIGNING OHP'S
- PRESENTATION

SELLING

- SALES VISITS
- TELE MARKETING
- OPEN PROGS
- PRESENTATIONS TO CLIENTS
- VISITS
- PROPOSAL WRITING

TUTOR

CREATING A JOB TREE
ACTIVITY IDEA

To create a job tree, take a blank sheet of paper (A3 is best), draw in a tree trunk and on to it write your job title.

Add to your tree truck the main branches, representing the chief elements of your job (probably about 6-8), annotating each branch accordingly (for instance, selling, team management, administration, etc).

Next, take each branch in turn and add smaller branches (or twigs) to elaborate on what each of the key elements of your job involves, ie: the tasks you do on a day-to-day basis. Again, you should annotate as you go along.

You now have a basic job tree.

CREATING A JOB TREE

ACTIVITY IDEA

The next phase in creating a job tree is to analyse your job in detail by annotating your tree in response to the instructions given below. Use different coloured pens or devise some sort of code to ensure you understand the tree when it is completed.

- Look at each of the key elements and decide what percentage of your time you spend on each. Note the figure on your tree beside each element.

- Which tasks do you like and dislike? Indicate on your tree the degree of liking or dislike in some way. (For instance, + + + for 'really like' and − − − for 'really dislike').

- Which tasks are regarded as important by either the organisation or your boss? Indicate this on the tree by the task, again indicating degree in some way.

- Looking at each of the tasks, how effective or skilled are you at them? Use a symbol to indicate the degree and annotate your tree.

- Now indicate where you need to develop by drawing a circle around the area.

- Finally, indicate if a particular area of your job needs developing by circling it in a different colour.

You should now have a complete job tree that represents your current job.

CREATING A JOB TREE

ANALYSIS

The whole purpose of a job tree is to provide you with a complete picture of your current job, to enable you to add to your analysis of your self-development needs.

Ask yourself the following questions and make notes:

- What patterns are emerging?
- What does it say about:
  - me?
  - my job?
  - my boss?
  - my organisation?
  - my likes and dislikes?
- What development issues and ideas are emerging?

Alternatively, you can discuss these questions with a learning partner or in a learning support group.

SELF-ANALYSIS

QUESTIONNAIRES

One common way of raising your self-awareness is by completing questionnaires. Whether the questionnaire is of the sort often found in magazines or the type you complete as part of a training exercise at work, the purpose is usually the same – namely, the opportunity for you to reflect on some aspect of your behaviour!

You may complete a questionnaire about your 'eating habits' or 'how you manage your love life' which would typically be found in some popular weekly and monthly magazines. Or, you may be attending a training course where you are asked to complete an inventory to assess your preferred style when working in teams. Having completed any questionnaire, you will be a little more self-aware!

SELF-ANALYSIS

QUESTIONNAIRES
ACTIVITY IDEA

You may find it useful to reflect back over the past few years (5 - 10) and focus on the various questionnaires that you have completed during training courses, in assessment centres, in performance reviews, etc.

● Get them out and have a look at them

● Identify what they are telling you about yourself

● Make notes in your learning log (you might like to categorise the topic areas for further, more detailed, analysis)

SKILLS/COMPETENCE REVIEW

One increasingly popular approach to self-analysis used by organisations is for individuals to undertake a skills or competence audit or review. Typically, this is done as part of either a training course or an organisation's performance review process. Either way, it can be extremely useful to help individuals focus on some or all of the following:

- Key skill strengths
- Key skill weaknesses
- Areas for personal development
- Areas where your job needs development
- Career or job focus areas

SELF-ANALYSIS

SKILLS/COMPETENCE REVIEW

On the following pages I have constructed a skills or competence review which is split into three key areas:

- Relationship skills
- Personal skills
- Business skills

You can use this inventory to review two things:

- How skilled you are in each area
- How necessary each area is to your particular job or career

In addition, you could also review which areas it will be necessary for you to work on in order to develop and advance further.

SKILLS/COMPETENCE REVIEW

INSTRUCTIONS

Competence Review

Think about each competence in terms of situations that occur across the major areas of your life, particularly work. Rate yourself using the following five-point scale:

1. **Not competent**   - an unused or untested area, or where you are totally lacking
2. **Some competence**   - a slight ability demonstrated in this area
3. **Fairly competent**   - an average ability demonstrated in this area
4. **Very competent**   - an above average ability demonstrated in this area
5. **Extremely competent** - regarded as an expert in this area

Job Importance Review

Think about your job, take each competence in turn and assess how important these are for success in your job (or life!):

1. **Not important**   - no ability necessary for success or effectiveness
2. **Some importance**   - some ability necessary to be successful and effective
3. **Fairly important**   - an average ability necessary to be successful and effective
4. **Very important**   - an above average ability necessary to be successful and effective
5. **Extremely important** - must be an expert in this area for success and effectiveness

SKILLS/COMPETENCE REVIEW

RELATIONSHIP SKILLS

COMPETENCE DESCRIPTION	COMPETENCE REVIEW	JOB IMPORTANCE REVIEW
Team Working - Co-operates and interacts with colleagues to develop a team-oriented approach to work	1 2 3 4 5	1 2 3 4 5
Influencing – Persuades convincingly, uses other's ideas constructively and gains commitment from others	1 2 3 4 5	1 2 3 4 5
Leadership - Takes responsibility for others, influencing and motivating them through own actions and words	1 2 3 4 5	1 2 3 4 5
Coaching - Helps others to develop by offering support, advice, guidance and resources	1 2 3 4 5	1 2 3 4 5
Delegating - Ensures commitment and individual accountability by delegating authority to others	1 2 3 4 5	1 2 3 4 5
Motivating - Understands and empathises with the needs of others in order to get the best out of them	1 2 3 4 5	1 2 3 4 5

SKILLS/COMPETENCE REVIEW

PERSONAL SKILLS

COMPETENCE DESCRIPTION	COMPETENCE REVIEW	JOB IMPORTANCE REVIEW
Self-management - Plans and organises effectively, making good use of time and prioritising	1 2 3 4 5	1 2 3 4 5
Communication - Communicates ideas and information in a clear, concise and open manner, both verbally and in writing	1 2 3 4 5	1 2 3 4 5
Listening - Is attentive to other's views and ideas and works to understand their point of view	1 2 3 4 5	1 2 3 4 5
Creativity - Uses originality and innovation in arriving at new solutions to old problems	1 2 3 4 5	1 2 3 4 5
Personal Effectiveness - Shows energy and commitment to making things happen, projects confidence and assertiveness in a wide variety of situations	1 2 3 4 5	1 2 3 4 5
Problem-solving & Decision-making - Analyses and works through problems in order to make effective decisions	1 2 3 4 5	1 2 3 4 5

SKILLS/COMPETENCE REVIEW

BUSINESS SKILLS

COMPETENCE DESCRIPTION	COMPETENCE REVIEW	JOB IMPORTANCE REVIEW
Commercial Awareness - Has a good understanding of business in general	1 2 3 4 5	1 2 3 4 5
Financial Awareness – Understands and uses key financial data in day-to-day work	1 2 3 4 5	1 2 3 4 5
IT Awareness – Is confident in using technology and understands how it contributes to the business	1 2 3 4 5	1 2 3 4 5
Strategic Awareness – Demonstrates understanding of the long-term and future direction of the business	1 2 3 4 5	1 2 3 4 5
Marketing Awareness – Understands the basic marketing principles and takes account of customer needs and market moves	1 2 3 4 5	1 2 3 4 5
Operations Management Awareness - Understands the various business processes that contribute to how a business operates effectively	1 2 3 4 5	1 2 3 4 5

SKILLS/COMPETENCE REVIEW

ANALYSIS

Having completed the skills/competence review, you may like to ask yourself some or all of the following questions and make appropriate notes in your learning log:

- What key strengths have I identified from the competence review?

- What are the most important areas identified in the job review inventory?

- What weaknesses have I identified from the competence review?

- What are the least important areas identified in the job review inventory?

- Are there any significant differences between the competence review and the job importance review, and what messages can I take from this?

- What additional competences/skills do I have to work on to be more effective in my current job?

- What competences/skills do I have to work on to develop or advance further for the future?

PERFORMANCE REVIEWS

Most of us who are in paid employment take part in some form of performance review process, usually on an annual basis. Sometimes, these experiences can be rather formal, focusing on past performance and future objectives, with your training and development and future career almost dealt with as an afterthought!

If you begin to look at this from a slightly different perspective - that of the self-developer - there may well be some interesting messages that you can extract from your various reviews over the past few years.

So, review the process, paperwork and memories for the following:

- Recurring messages about strengths/weaknesses
- The types of job objectives you have been set on a year-by-year basis
  (Were they enjoyable or a chore? What does this tell you?)
- Training needs identified - those met and not met
- Career development issues discussed (What has happened about these?)

Again, note in your learning log any important points emerging.

CASE STUDY: MARY'S STORY

'Against all odds' – were Mary's own words when I met her to discuss her story. Why?

Mary was one of 10 children born in Manchester in the late 1930s. Though experiencing many school changes, she managed to pass her 11+. However, she was made to leave school at 15 to work in a cotton mill where she stayed for two years. She then moved south and worked in various unskilled jobs until she married and started a family. While raising her family Mary always worked – in a sweet shop, as a cleaner and as a dinner lady in a school, and then various jobs on the housekeeping and catering staff at Ashridge Management College.

Mary has worked hard all her life, but what makes her special from a self-managed development perspective? The defining moment for Mary came when her husband died of cancer.

CASE STUDY: MARY'S STORY

Having nursed her husband through his illness, Mary offered her services to the local hospice to help other people who were in a similar predicament. Her offer was rejected because she had no 'qualifications'!

It was at this stage that Mary decided to do something about her development. She took several courses in typing, computer skills and alternative therapy. It was in this area that Mary finally found her niche.

Not content with short courses and wanting to 'show the hospice she too could be qualified', Mary embarked on a part-time Introduction to Counselling course which lasted for three years. Owing to her lack of formal education and a mild form of dyslexia, Mary found the course challenging, particularly the lectures and homework. The support of her course tutor was absolutely vital in encouraging her to keep going.

CASE STUDY: MARY'S STORY

At the end of this course Mary needed 100 hours' practical work in order to qualify for the diploma. She again offered her services to the hospice and was yet again turned down. This, Mary said, 'knocked her back quite a bit'. The hospice wanted her to do their own qualification.

Having got over yet another set-back, she approached the local Elderly Care Centre manager who gave Mary the opportunity to gain her practical experience within the unit. The service Mary provided during this time proved to be both invaluable and pioneering in its nature. So, the unit manager decided to lobby her bosses to get funds to pay Mary for her services. Her first payment was made on 1 December 1996.

Mary continues to work in the unit, both as a counsellor and as someone who constantly looks at new services to offer.

CASE STUDY: MARY'S STORY
KEY SELF-DEVELOPMENT ISSUES

What makes Mary's story interesting from a self-managed development perspective?

- Her ability to overcome so many obstacles throughout her life, to move on and use different life experiences as learning opportunities
- Recognition that formal education does not equal intelligence or ability
- Her ability to formulate her goals and her persistence to achieve them
- Recognising and accepting that people can help in the process
- Having the guts to take risks and to challenge the status quo in order to achieve her dreams

Mary is a fascinating woman, who has overcome many obstacles in her life in order to grow and develop into areas she finds interesting. She has taken many risks along the way and has suffered many set-backs but has always come back fighting. She is a true self-developer who analyses, reflects and plans. And, if an opportunity does not present itself to her, she creates the opportunity!

NOTES

REFLECTION

WHY REFLECT?

Having spent some time on self-analysis, it is now important to spend some time reflecting and reviewing.

The purpose of reflection is to review your perceptions in order to be aware of new possibilities, so that you have more choices in the future. If you do not reflect then, perhaps, the following quote summarises what will happen:

> *"If you continue to do what you've always done, then you'll continue to get what you've always got!"* Anon

Perhaps this is okay for some people, but if you are interested in self-managed development then you are probably not totally happy with what you've already got!

DON'T WAIT FOR A CRISIS!

Sadly, many of us leave reflection until faced with some crisis in our lives - for instance, redundancy, divorce, serious illness. I believe that regular reflection as part of a process where you focus on...

- Making sense of the self-analysis you have done
- Where you are now
- Where you want to go in the future

...is invaluable as part of your self-managed development process.

REFLECTION

SHARE YOUR THOUGHTS

While this process can be done on your own, it is often more effective to share your thoughts and views with others. Spending some time working with one of the people in your learning network - or, indeed, working with your learning support group - to help you focus and gain clarity, can be a very rewarding part of the whole self-managed development experience.

A major element of this part of the process can also involve getting feedback from others to:

- Check your own self-perceptions
- Confirm others' perceptions
- Gain feedback on specific issues

REFLECTION

WHAT TO ASK YOURSELF

Reviewing your self-analysis and self-perceptions, in particular to check where you are now, is, perhaps, the first stage of any reflection process.

Asking yourself the questions listed below, and noting the answers in your learning log, will help you to summarise where you are now! You may want to refer back to previous notes in your learning log in order to answer some of the questions.

- What are my current roles in life?
  - Work role or job?
  - Other roles (eg: parent, partner, football coach, PTA chairperson)?
- What are my important strengths?
- What particular skills am I good at?

- What do I enjoy doing in work and life?
- What are my major weaknesses?
- What have been my major achievements?
- What have I been disappointed about?
- What limitations are there in my job/life?

REFLECTION

ASK OTHERS FOR THEIR VIEWS

Summarising your self-perceptions of where you are now is, however, only one part of the process. It is also important to check what others (eg: work colleagues, family and friends) think about you, in order to get a full picture of where you are now.

But before asking others for feedback, think about and note down how you expect they will answer these questions:

- What adjectives best describe me?
- What are my greatest strengths/weaknesses?

You will now be able to compare their actual answers with your own self-perceptions. Are there similarities or significant differences? What key messages are emerging from this?

REFLECTION

ACTIVITY

You should now have a pretty good picture of your own self-perceptions and some thoughts about those of others. However, checking out these perceptions and thoughts before you decide where you want to go is invaluable.

So, examine all your notes and thoughts so far and look for patterns and key issues that you would like to examine with others.

ADVICE ON GETTING FEEDBACK

Getting feedback from others can be a highly-charged emotional experience! The way you receive any feedback can determine whether or not you will ever get any again. Here are a few tips:

DO   ask people you trust and respect for feedback.

DO   be honest and open - let them know that you have FEELINGS!

DO   remember that face-to-face feedback is a big step for most people.

DO   ask open questions – Who? When? Why? How? What?

DO   listen fully to answers or comments.

DO   use active listening - checking understanding.

DO   focus on specific issues you want to know about, rather than on all aspects of your behaviour/personality at once.

ADVICE ON GETTING FEEDBACK

Remember, you wanted the feedback. If someone has been good enough to agree to give you feedback, then make sure that you:

DON'T   be judgmental - accept the answers and review later.

DON'T   make excuses for answers or comments given.

DON'T   be defensive.

DON'T   argue.

DON'T   let your body language send out mixed messages.

DON'T   analyse the data - try to understand it.

STRUCTURING FEEDBACK

Getting feedback from others is not only an emotional experience, it is also a complex one. In order to make the process easier, on both yourself and the feedback provider, it is often useful to adopt a structure.

One approach might be to ask the person to write down one or two things s/he thinks you should:

- Do less of
- Do more of
- Do differently

This can then be followed by a discussion on the topics raised, at which the feedback provider puts forward the topics and you clarify to ensure you understand.

Any feedback using this process will depend, to a large extent, upon the knowledge the person has of you in various situations.

REFLECTION

STRUCTURING FEEDBACK

Another approach to structuring feedback is to plan out particular aspects of your behaviour that you would like feedback about, and then ask the feedback provider the following question:

Can you please give me feedback about my skills as:

- A listener?
- A chairperson?
- An interviewer?
- A coach?
- A team member?
- A team leader?
- A boss?

(Add other categories to the list, as appropriate.)

This process could be linked to the previous one by adding: 'Perhaps you could indicate the things I should do more of, do less of and do differently'.

TAKE CHARGE OF YOUR FEEDBACK

Remember, you're in charge of any feedback you receive. It can give you pleasure or pain and the many points in between! In the final analysis, you decide what to do about the feedback:

- **Adapt and adjust**
  or
- **Ignore it!**

You should also remember :

> *"I can't tell you what you are,*
> *but you can't tell me what I see!"*
> *Anon*

VISUALISE THE FUTURE

Another important aspect of reflection is to focus on the future.

One way of focusing on the future is to use a technique called visualisation. In looking to the future, you should focus on both career and personal aims.

Dreaming about or visualising where you would like to be, what you would like to be doing at a point in the future, can be a very useful and enjoyable activity.

REFLECTION

HOW TO VISUALISE

Visualisation is a creative process involving you in dreaming about the future and what you want. The following guidelines will help you in the process:

- Work in a comfortable, quiet and private environment
- Make sure that you have a block of time (about an hour at least) and that you won't be interrupted
- Perhaps, play some quiet music that you enjoy and find easy to listen to
- Sit back, relax and let your mind wander about your life/job/future
- Remember to focus on the detail as well as the big picture
- Perhaps, focus on one of the following areas:
  - What would my dream job be?
  - Where would I like to be in 1/5/10 years' time?
  - What things would I like to achieve during my lifetime?

HOW TO VISUALISE

There are, of course, some traps to avoid when visualising. For instance, you might begin and then think some (or all) of the following:

All of the above are
legitimate reasons why visualisation is hard. The important thing to remember is that if you start to evaluate during the process, you will negate the outcome.

REFLECTION

HOW TO VISUALISE

ACTIVITY IDEA

Try the following three-stage activity:

- Firstly, do some personal visualisation following the guidelines suggested earlier
- Secondly, note down your thoughts and ideas in your learning log
- Thirdly, work with one of your learning partners to share and explore your thoughts and ideas, in order to begin to make sense of them and to incorporate them into your self-development plans

WHY NOT

Remember what George Bernard Shaw said:

> "You see things; and you say, 'Why?'.
> But I dream things that never were; and I say,
> 'Why not?'"

LOOK BACKWARDS & FORWARDS

Reflection is a bit like looking in the rear-view mirror before driving off!

So, before you move onto action planning for the future it is always valuable to spend some time, either alone or, perhaps, in discussion with others, to:

- Look backwards
- Dream of the future

ACTION PLANNING

HOW AN ACTION PLAN HELPS

The real challenge to the self-developer is to make the transition from analysis and reflection to action.

A good self-development action plan will help you to focus on:

- What you want to achieve
- How you will achieve it
- Who could help you in the process
- Any barriers or constraints you might encounter
- When you want to achieve it

PLAN PITFALLS

Preparing an action plan may seem relatively easy. There are, however, certain pitfalls, which you should be aware of:

- Too many goals
- Goals that are too ambitious – remember this is about developing yourself, **not** impressing others
- Vague goals
- Unrealistic timescales
- Making it too hard – remember it's okay for learning to be fun!

GETTING ACHIEVABLE GOALS

The most challenging part of any action plan is setting sufficiently challenging yet achievable goals.

For instance, it is not enough to say 'I want to get fit'. Why not? Because this does not cover:

- How you will do it
- How you will measure success
- The timescales
- Others involved to help

PLAN COMPONENTS

In order to give yourself the best possible chance to succeed, in whatever goal/s you choose, it is best to divide-up the overall goal into manageable chunks.

Each action plan should consist of:

- An overall goal
- A set of actions which are clear, measurable and outcome focused
- A timescale to help measure progress
- Details of others involved
- How you will measure success

ACTION PLANNING

YOUR LEARNING LOG

One approach you may like to take is to structure an action planning section in your learning log, along the following lines:

Overall goal ▸ To get fit by taking part in regular exercise!

Action	Timescale
● Join a gym	● By end of week
● Book a fitness assessment	● By end of week
● Work out a personal exercise programme to suit my needs	● For a 6-week period
● Exercise at least 3 times a week	● 3 times a week
● Reassess fitness	● 6 weeks from start date
● Develop a new exercise routine	● After 6 weeks
● Build exercise into weekly plans	● As a routine

Others involved
● Fitness instructor   ● Friends and family for support

Success measures
● Incremental improvements in fitness levels every 6 weeks
● Interest level maintained by varying exercise routine
● Regularly exercising (3 times per week)

TYPES OF GOALS

This relatively simple action planning technique can be applied to any type of goal:

- Personal
- Career
- Work

The important thing to remember about action planning and, in particular, about achieving your self-development goals, is that **you** must have goal clarity and the motivation to achieve the goal.

COMMITMENT & MOTIVATION

One way of measuring your personal commitment and motivation is to assess each goal you set yourself according to a) its importance to you and b) how clear you are about the steps you need to take. Use this matrix as a measuring tool:

High	**2** Low importance High clarity	**3** High importance High clarity
Commitment	**1** Low importance Low clarity	**4** High importance Low clarity
Low		**High**
	Motivation	

 Typically, successful goals will tend to fall in quadrant 3!

ACTION PLANNING

ACTIVITY IDEA

A useful approach for successful action planning is to:

- Decide on your goals and write them down in your learning log (remember, not too many – give yourself a fighting chance of success!)
- Assess each goal using the matrix on the previous page
- Develop your detailed action plans using the suggested structure or some other approach which suits you

FINAL WORD

*"Always bear in mind
that your own resolution to succeed is more
important than any other one thing."*
Abraham Lincoln

SUMMARY

KEY POINTS OF BOOK

The following key points summarise the main messages of this book:

- **Create a development log** — a recording system to suit your own particular needs

- **Focus on your objective** — have a reason to develop: job, life, a particular skill, etc (write it down!)

- **Develop a personal profile** — get to know yourself, ask yourself questions (many of which are contained in this book) and note down the answers in your log

- **Do a personal SWOT analysis**

- **Complete questionnaires** — these can help you to make sense of many different aspects of your life by providing a structure and framework

KEY POINTS OF BOOK

- **List your achievements** — what you have been proud of in your life
- **Focus on how you learn** — we all learn in different ways; consider how you learn best
- **Ask others** — get feedback from other people
- **Focus on the present** — take stock of where you are now
- **Focus on the future** — look ahead; think about all aspects of your life
- **Develop your self-managed development strategy** — write it down; have some goals

Remember, Your Development is in Your Hands

SELF-MANAGED DEVELOPMENT

FURTHER READING

'Signposts For Success' *by Fiona Elsa Dent, Robert MacGregor & Stefan Wills, Pitman 1994*

'Your Best Year Yet' *by Jinny S. Ditzler, Thorsons 1994*

'Wisboroughs - Make A New Start With A Fresh View On Life' *by Chrissie McGinn & Richard Hewitt, Wessex Aquarian Publications 1995*

'A Manager's Guide To Self Development' *by Mike Pedlar, John Burgoyne & Tom Boydell, McGraw Hill 1986*

'Build Your Own Rainbow, A Workbook For Career And Life Management' *by Brian Hopson & Mike Scally, Lifeskills Publishing Group 1991*

About the Author

Fiona Elsa Dent, MSc. MIPD
Fiona is a Programme & Client Director at Ashridge Management
College where she specialises in the organisational behaviour area.
In her role as trainer and coach she helps people to develop a
wide range of personal, interpersonal and relationship skills.

Her belief in the whole process of self-managed development has
led her to write several articles on the topic and to co-author
another book 'Signposts For Success'. She also runs workshops
to help individuals understand the process and how to do it.

Prior to joining Ashridge, Fiona held management development
and training positions in The Automobile Association,
Equitable Life Assurance Society and The Target Group.

Contact
Fiona runs her own consultancy and can be contacted at:
16 The Spinney
Beaconsfield
Bucks. HP9 1SB
Telephone: 01442 843491
E-mail: fiona.dent@ashridge.org.uk

ORDER FORM

Your details

Name _____

Position _____

Company _____

Address _____

_____

_____

Telephone _____

Facsimile _____

E-mail _____

VAT No. (EC companies) _____

Your Order Ref _____

Please send me:

		No. copies
The <u>Self-Managed Development</u>	Pocketbook	☐
The _____	Pocketbook	☐
The _____	Pocketbook	☐
The _____	Pocketbook	☐
The _____	Pocketbook	☐

Order by Post
MANAGEMENT POCKETBOOKS LTD
14 EAST STREET ALRESFORD HAMPSHIRE SO24 9EE UK

Order by Phone, Fax or Internet
Telephone: +44 (0)1962 735573
Facsimile: +44 (0)1962 733637
E-mail: pocketbks@aol.com
Web: www.pocketbook.co.uk

Customers in USA should contact:
Stylus Publishing, LLC, 22883 Quicksilver Drive,
Sterling, VA 20166-2012
Telephone: 703 661 1581 or 800 232 0223
Facsimile: 703 661 1501 E-mail: styluspub@aol.com

MANAGEMENT POCKETBOOKS